Seasons of the Yellowstone

Grand Canyon

Mammoth

Norris Jct.

Canyon

HAYDEN VALLEY

GRAND CANYON OF THE YELLOWSTONE

Tower Jct.

Fishing Bridge

Yellowstone Lake

Lamar River

Yellowstone R.

poets, writers, artists, and photographers for generations.

It is along the buttes of the Yellowstone's Grand Canyon that the Sheepeater Indians, no longer in existence, once lived. Fearful of the geysers slightly west that would have warmed them in the bitter Yellowstone winters, the Sheepeaters eked out a ragged living hunting bighorn sheep with obsidian-tipped arrows. By comparison, sixty miles to the north, Crow Indians had a sumptuous life hunting buffalo, deer, and elk on the banks of the Yellowstone River in and around the more temperate Paradise Valley.

From the Grand Canyon of the Yellowstone, the river continues a tumultuous course, picking up volume from the Lamar and Gardner rivers before boiling out of Black Canyon at the park's northwestern gateway community of Gardiner. It is here that tourists, hunters, and adventurers came in the mid-to-late 19th century to visit what was commonly called "John Colter's Hell." A member of the Lewis and Clark expedition, Colter later explored what is now Yellowstone Park. His journals describing and depicting Mammoth Hot Springs, the majesty of the region, and its other geothermal activity were initially met with widespread disbelief by the press and the populace "back in the states." But by the 1860s a rough toll road from Livingston to the gold fields of Emigrant Gulch was extended to Gardiner. And the wilderness area that would become Yellowstone

The Grand Canyon of the Yellowstone River.

Solitude and solace are two things the Yellowstone offers the reflective angler in abundance.

National Park became the playground of wealthy hunters and seasonal visitors, complete with vacation homes. The toll road is now a hiking trail and its former owner, Yankee Jim, is said to have flashed President Theodore Roosevelt the international symbol of contempt when Roosevelt passed through to dedicate the world's first national park in 1872.

From Gardiner, the Yellowstone River, like a freshly broken mount, settles into an uneasy trot for thirteen miles. This is a fine stretch of river that offers superb fishing for cutthroats in riffles, glides, chutes, and numerous creek mouths. Much of this stretch is "technical water" and should be avoided by novice oarsmen.

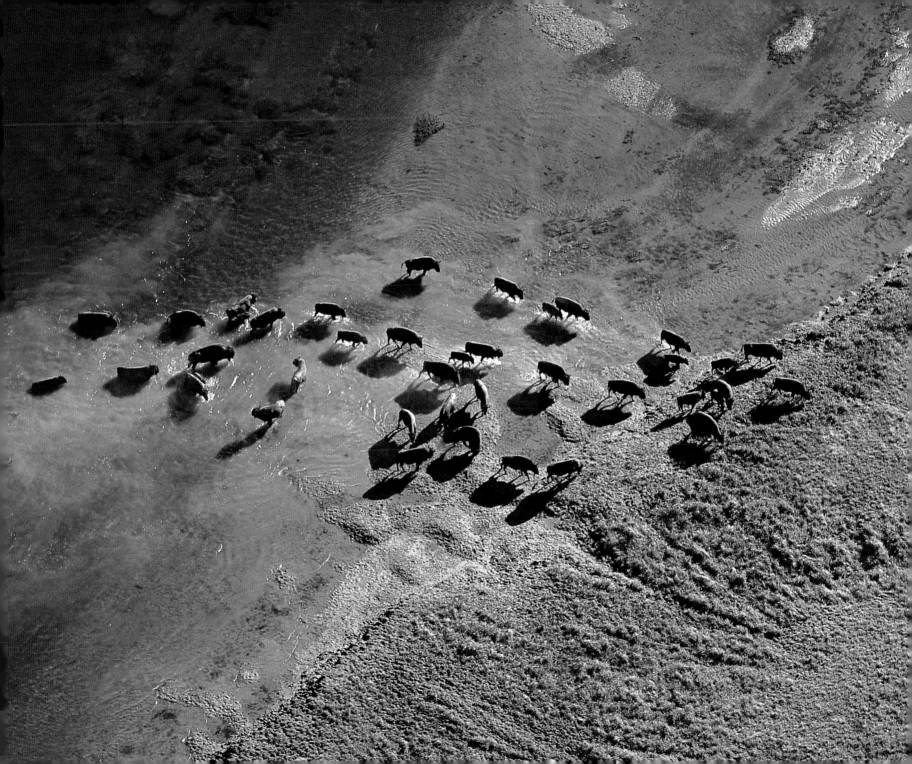

wave. Through his New York contacts, Bailey enlisted early flyfishing writers and pioneers, such as Joe Brooks and Lee Wulff, to focus attention on the sport of flyfishing and on the Yellowstone.

But fishing the Yellowstone then was very different from a day of fishing now, according to Bailey's son, John, who has managed the shop since Dan Bailey's death in 1982. "We used Army surplus rubber rafts then," John Bailey says with a laugh. "Later we started using aluminum Jon boats. We didn't fish from the boats much. And we didn't have much access. We'd float from one bridge to the next."

The Yellowstone River's 40-year guide emeritus, Donnie Williams, agrees. "I remember my first raft with

Dan Bailey's fly shop in Livingston is a flyfishing icon. John Bailey carries on the shop's tradition.

my homemade rowing frame," he says wistfully. But what early guides lacked in watercraft quality was more than compensated by the Yellowstone's quality. Said Williams, "We'd never see anyone on the river for days. And

As with most large western rivers, the drift boat is the workhorse of the Yellowstone, getting anglers to stretches that are unreachable by wading.

and they'd be so thick that they'd cover fence posts, making them look twice the size." And, he added, "Twenty-fish days were average on the Yellowstone back then, and it wasn't uncommon to have 60-fish days, all on dry flies. There wasn't much nymph fishing done then."

By comparison, nowadays a battalion of outfitters and guides drift the Yellowstone in sleek MacKenzie drift boats. Public access sites dot the riverbanks at 10-mile intervals and clients arrive at the take-outs precisely when expected so that dinner reservations won't be missed. The fishing for stream-bred wild trout is still superb, although a 6-pound trout is now the exception rather than the rule.

To maintain the fishery in the last half of the 20th century, the Yellow-

there were lots of 2- to 6-pound fish, and even lots of 7-pounders." Of the famous salmonfly hatches of the 1960s, which are now starting to come back, Williams said, "The salmonflies would start in Springdale

stone River has faced a number of environmental challenges, but none as singular and profound as the proposed Allens Spur Dam. An engineer's dream as far back as 1904, damming the Yellowstone at the Allens Spur narrows, the point south of Livingston where the Absaroka and Gallatin mountains are separated by a mere half-mile and the Yellowstone River, was a serious proposal in the late 1960s. According to Corps of Engineers plans, the dam would have created a huge reservoir in Paradise Valley, water to be used for coal-burning power plants downstream and jet stream mining of Montana's huge coal deposits.

Battle lines were drawn and a bitter and prolonged fight over the proposed dam ensued. Although

Bisected by the Yellowstone River, the scenic Paradise Valley, once a broad sweep of cattle range, is now a magnet for residential development.

many people contributed, it was Dan Bailey who stood at the center of the fray, enlisting the help of academicians, scientists, environmentalists from what was then an embryonic field, state Fish, Wildlife & Parks

During the consecutive flood years of 1996 and 1997, the low-tech sand bag saved many homes along the Yellowstone's course.

calling for minimum in-stream river flows for the benefit of public use. Second, a similar earthen dam in Wyoming's Grand Tetons gave way, with catastrophic results. Together with public resistance to the Allens Spur Dam, the proposal collapsed.

Nearly 25 years later, John Bailey continues the fight to keep the Yellowstone undammed. "It's not a dead issue," he insists. But instead of cross-river dams, Bailey and others believe the current trend of building berms and levees in the river's flood-plain is an equal threat. "If you can do that, you can build a dam," John Bailey argues. "We now have no defensible position if another dam were to be proposed." The Greater Yellowstone Coalition's (GYC) Dennis Glick agrees. "Berms and

Department employees, anglers, the press, and the public. Two nearly concurrent events helped Dan Bailey win the day. First and most import-antly, the Montana Constitution was redrawn in 1973 to include language

SPRING

IT'S NOT HARD TO TELL WHEN spring comes to the Yellowstone River, whether you are an angler or not. It's just that from an angler's perspective the difference is that you start digging around in your fly boxes for dry flies that you haven't used for some time. And you realize with a sinking certainty that you should have spent a bit more time at the vise over the winter spinning up a few more suitable dry flies. The bedraggled and shop-worn selection left over from last season will have to do for now.

Come spring, the diamond-hard winter gloss of the Yellowstone and its environs softens in late March or early

Spring on the Yellowstone is the time for "small stuff"—midges, golden stones, and all manner of emergers.

April, when a bona fide 70-degree breeze wafts from the southeast. Wherever you are in the region, winter-bowed backs straighten and hands are raised to feel the warmth as if in disbelief or thanks. Sure, warm

Chinook winds have stayed Mother Nature's wintry hand at most of the season's darkest moments. But this spring breeze is the genuine article, a lithe and silver flute note with a written guarantee.

Frozen as hard as a bullet, the Yellowstone's flora is unable to respond. Or it does so inscrutably. But not the river. Shelf ice that a week earlier nearly spanned even the fastest riffles and runs breaks off in enormous chunks and drifts away. Massive snow banks on the river's edge that stood for months like steroid-pumped bodybuilders quickly turn to rotting snow and skeletal ice. And the water itself, pewter and sullen, takes on a visibly bright new mood as its temperature slowly rises from the grave-cold grip of winter.

Slate drakes, both spinners and duns, are among the first big mayflies to appear on the Yellowstone in the spring.

The Yellowstone's trout, too, respond to this annual transformation. The last of the spring-spawning rainbows are still full of intent on their redds. But the browns, cutthroats, and jack rainbows get into a pugnacious mood. They're just waiting for a good fight — the chance to break a chilled graphite tip or snap a 4X tippet just for the hell of it. But for the angler, breaking the fishing habits of winter, while seemingly easy, isn't. It's a while before you realize that the egg patterns, bead-head whatevers, and San Juan Worms — flies used all winter both because they work and for their deniability — are not what the trout want now. It takes a moment, a day or more of realization that the tiny flotilla before you is

spring *Baetis* duns intermixed with a few big brown drakes, and that the trout are actually taking them off the surface! Six months ago the hatch was matched immediately and without hesitation. Now it's done as a leap of faith with a shaky hand.

It is such that spring comes to the Yellowstone, slowly but inexorably. Though it takes a while for the vegetation to respond to the increasing warmth and longer days, respond it does. From the sentinel cottonwood groves that line its banks to the impenetrable helix of wild roses that beckon yet protect the river's secret places, another spring raises its unlined face to the high-desert sun. Thus the angler's stage is set.

Come early spring, I can't resist a visit to Dan Bailey's Fly Shop in downtown Livingston, a town of 7,000 hard by the Yellowstone's banks and the film site of what's locally called "the movie," Robert Redford's depiction of the book, *A River Runs Through It*. I don't come to Bailey's to talk winter fishing or to buy the odd hook, brass bead, or feather. I come to see the hatch board, a hand-written public notice of which flies, natural and artificial, the trout are taking. The hatch board lists all the usual suspects: Sawyer Pheasant Tails, So and So's midge emergers and duns, caddis pupae and emergers, and Gold-Ribbed Hare's Ears — standard fare. But for the first time the board lists *Baetis* duns and March Browns. Since I've been fishing them for a week or more the new entries don't surprise me. It's more a matter that

their annual arrival is affirmed by the printed word, albeit the slanted and scrawly printing of the shop manager. A rite of spring, if you will.

For decades, Livingston was a railroad community that drew its

Despite the harsh realities of a Montana winter, inhabitants of the Yellowstone region such as this elk cow and newborn calf find a way to endure.

The flood of 1997 saw the Yellowstone's flows swell to a record 33,000 cubic feet per second, more than twenty times the river's normal flow.

breath first from behemoth steam locomotives and later from the cloying belch of diesel engines. Burlington–Northern relocated in the mid-1980s and only a remnant of the city's railroad heritage remains.

Its many bars, cheek-by-jowl houses, and frontier mien does not immediately identify it as one of the West's finest flyfishing destinations. But it is and long has been. Livingston is just recently, with the conspicuous absence of the railroad, rather flinchingly coming to grips with its new identity. The town now largely draws its sustenance from the credit cards of visiting anglers. And in the decade since the railroad left town, there has arisen a battalion of outfitters, guides, and other full- and part-time trout bums who have forsaken much or little for the region's final Gold Rush — the Yellowstone and its trout.

When my aging Suburban settles with an audible wheeze into the dusty parking lot a few miles south of town, I see one of the full-timers standing thigh-deep in the river. A few patches of snow remain and a breeze with an edge of winter greets me as I roll the window down to watch. The angler casts, mends, and dead-drifts his offering in a metronomic rhythm. Every few casts he takes a careful step or two downstream, down the run. I know him by his signature army surplus field jacket, bulging fly vest, and his angling intensity, which is nothing short of that of a great blue heron. Mesmerized, I jolt upright in my seat minutes later when the angler strikes, setting a large 'bow in his rod. The rod bucks as the unseen trout powers downriver and the angler takes a few steps backward, into shallower water. After a challenging fight, he brings a spring-bright rainbow of a couple pounds to hand and releases it

with practiced agility. With a glance my way, he waves. I return the slight gesture but he's already false-casting while wading back into the run.

After watching the scene unfold I'm anxious to get out there, and so is Sam, my Labrador retriever and my hunting and fishing pal. With my rod strung and waders hitched up, I head for the bottom of the run. It's a 300-yard side channel of the main river that doesn't get a lot of pressure, especially during the off-season months. It's mid-April, and only the most precocious of green shoots are in evidence. Otherwise it could be late fall, except that there's a whiff of spring's unique fecundity on the breeze. From habit I watch the water, bank, and bushes for a long few minutes to detect any insect activity,

Montana's enlightened stream-access laws provide many places for anglers to fish the Yellowstone River.

A winter resident of the Yellowstone, the bald eagle patrols the river's banks in numbers and seems to know that it's top gun.

I'm startled by one of our winter residents as we clear the bushes. A lone bald eagle flushes high in a nearby cottonwood, indignant as only hunting raptors can be. The big bird obviously had designs on the rising trout, too. The source of its indignation was, rightly, that it was there first. The eagle wheels to the opposite bank and settles on a high perch, giving me a full frontal view as it focuses its laser beams of intolerance on us intruders. As a nod to flyfishing etiquette, I briefly entertain the idea of yielding the run to the magnificent bird. But hell, I'm a predator too. I move into casting position.

The trout are obviously rising to an emerger, but there's nothing to indicate what it may be. After changing flies three times and getting steadfast

terrestrial or aquatic. Nothing is evident, but a couple of nice trout are rising in a bankside slick downstream. Sam sees the action too, and we follow a convenient deer trail through thick willow bushes and cane to get downstream of the porpoising trout.

Summer

UMMER ON THE YELLOWSTONE RIVER is as unique as the river itself. While many of the nation's trout rivers have already seen their best hatches, the Yellowstone is just getting started. Runoff, which kept the river high and unfishable through May, June, and much of July, is tapering off. The river is dropping and clearing by the day, grasshoppers are buzzing in the heat of the long summer days, and the trout are on the fin.

It's a hectic and exciting time in the Yellowstone region, and the river is the centerpiece. Fly shops from Big Timber to Livingston to Gardiner are jammed with visiting anglers who have nurtured winter dreams of big, wild western trout.

Cliff jumping in Yellowstone Park.

Rental cars, motor homes, and other vehicles bearing license plates from such distant places as Florida, Alaska, and Maine stream off Interstate 90, bound for Yellowstone National Park or one of the many and varied guest ranches, lodges, motels, and campgrounds that dot the region. Many come to fish, some are here to ride horses, some come to hike the high country, some want to simply relax. But all will be awed and touched in various ways by the sheer majesty and scope of the Yellowstone region.

From the river, the Absaroka Mountains (pronounced *ab-sorka*) concede scant valley floor before towering to 10,921 feet at their highest point as they flank the river from Yellowstone Park to Livingston.

Under the impossibly clear, blue, and endless Montana summer skies, the snow-capped Absarokas overwhelm mind, eye, and imagination. If the ocean has the ability to calm and wash away one's problems, the Absarokas have the ability to put everything in perspective.

Flanking the Yellowstone River to the west is the Gallatin Range. Though actually higher than the Absarokas by 71 feet, by comparison the Gallatins appear to be rolling hills until they bare and flex their muscles on the outskirts of Yellowstone Park. At the foot of each range, paved roads parallel the river. The vehicles traveling these roads in Paradise Valley to get to Yellowstone Park, trailheads to the high country or to the river, appear absurdly Lilliputian

Wading is an effective way to fish the Yellowstone River, but it's an underutilized tactic, especially among visiting anglers.

against the mountain backdrops.

Some say that Paradise Valley may be the sum of all superlatives when it comes to its Rocky Mountain grandeur. I agree. There are few river valleys in Montana that compare. But like them all, to see the Yellowstone region from its finest perspective and to touch its feral soul, the Yellowstone River itself is that perspective and soul source. As immutable as the mountains that flank it, the Yellowstone neither asked nor gave any quarter over the ages. It's more likely that, vice-versa, the Gallatins and Absarokas yielded to the course of this mighty river. Although tame in the summer, during spring runoff the Yellowstone eats ill-sited houses like penny candy, downs and mangles huge cottonwood trees on its banks, and redistributes rock, sand, and sediment in the millions of tons like a giant rooting beast. Wading or floating its waters in the summer is to touch its becalmed soul. And there is no better way to do that than from a drift boat.

The MacKenzie drift boat, a distant relative of the Maine river dory and the Adirondack guide boat, is perfectly suited to the Yellowstone River. This oar-powered craft with its wide beam and smooth, rockered bottom is a marvel in the hands of an experienced oarsman. And its quiet passage goes almost unnoticed by fish and wildlife. I've often drifted by within casting distance of deer, bears, eagles, and the occasional moose who take only casual note of the 16-foot boat. Seated at the oars or standing in

fly in a nondescript run along the bank? For me, the answer to each question is no. The white noise of daily life would have blunted my senses. But not in predator mode.

It's high noon now. The sound of grasshoppers clicking their wings has increased with the heat of the day. The bright sun is bearing hard on the river, and even wearing sunglasses you have to squint to follow your fly. The guide's soft drinks stopped quenching your thirst in the humidity-free mountain air an hour ago and you've switched to water. You've landed five trout, three of them the biggest you've ever caught. The knee locks are starting to chafe and a nettlesome blister has formed on the thumb of your casting hand. You want to stretch your legs, then sit in the shade to rest your back and other parts of your protesting body. But you're too strung out on the opiates of wilderness, of trout, of being off the leash, and you don't want to miss a take. "Getting hungry?" the guide asks.

The 65-degree water of the Yellowstone is pleasant as you wade into the back channel to fish while your guide prepares lunch. Unlike the river, it's a quiet place, willow-lined and cool — more like a remote stream unto itself, not connected to the great river. The big husks of long-hatched stoneflies still cling to the sun-baked cobble, whose interstitial mud bears the fresh tracks of heron, deer, and something big that you can't identify. A furtive glance around for the track-maker gives form and texture to the concept of "wild country."

Caddisflies cling to vegetation along the Yellowstone before returning to the river to mate and lay their eggs.

Among the Yellowstone's many wild trout, there's likely to be one bruiser looking to tangle with you.

From there, you get pantheistic or proprietary about "your run." Either attitude works. But the hopper doesn't, so you tie on 5X tippet and a small Adams Parachute. On the first drift along the far bank the big head of a cutthroat appears inches below your fly. The fish casually and confidently opens its mouth, closes it on the fly, and disappears beneath the surface. It's almost too classic and, awed, you almost forget to set the hook. But you do. And the big cutt flashes, turns, and heads for the end of the run and the freedom of the open river. Events now happen in freeze-frame and cascades, all seemingly a step ahead of you. You stumble over the cobble to keep up with the trout's downstream run, using the resistance of the fish as a counterbalance. Even with your progress afoot, the reel is losing line to the trout at an astonishing rate. In your peripheral vision you note with a fleeting measure of confidence that your guide has materialized at the end of the run, net in hand. As if the fly line you regained wound around your heart, each of the trout's dogged runs are physically painful. You want this trout. Interminable minutes later he's yours, 20 inches of wild Yellowstone cutthroat that transcends itself in beauty and value beyond all reason. Numbed and with trembling hands, you pose for a couple of photos with the fish, release it, and accept the guide's handshake and congratulations.

"My God!" you think.

"Let's eat," the guide says.

AUTUMN

AUTUMN IS UNDOUBTEDLY the most textured time of year on the Yellowstone and in the region. The rolling boil of tourist season reduces to a simmer right after Labor Day. In its place is the high and lonesome call of the wapiti as they prepare for the breeding season. In counterpoint is the raspy keening of the red-tailed hawk, anxious to head south for the season. The first frost is not far distant, evidenced by the brass-bright summer sun that now has the muted timbre more of woodwind than trumpet. The change of season is on the wind, too. And although still verdant, the river bottom is musty with the decadence of fall.

The summer visitors are gone, the trout have been cast over all summer. You've got to be good at the game to score now.

The supple willows now rattle in the wind, and here and there the first veins of crimson, gold, and brown belie the hopeful promise of endless summer in the leaves of the highest trees. Within a month, crisp nights and a snow or two will leave no doubt in mind or eye that autumn holds sway. But it will happen by degrees, in stages that are well understood by game, fish, and fowl.

By mid-October the face and mood of the Yellowstone has changed. The temperate days when small mayflies hatch and the trout feed on top are fewer. On such days, the trout will still take a small hopper pattern, but only from memory and tentatively, without the gusto and confidence of summer past. The water temperature has dropped by at least ten degrees, replacing casual wet-wading with the careful, neoprene-clad wading of fall. A summer dunking is refreshing. In late autumn it can be and has been fatal. On the river's banks, the cottonwoods, alders, cane, and willows stand gray and skeletal, stripped of leaf and hue, victims of the pre-winter winds that rake the region. It's a distracting and disquieting change, this unceremonious disrobing, an ultimate reality check to splinters of psyche still clad in shorts and T-shirts.

Few drift boats ride the Yellowstone now. The visiting summer anglers are gone. And many local flyfishers have switched from rod to gun to harvest a bird or two on the wing from the region's abundancy. Others are drawn to the Yellowstone

River's rich neighbors — the spring creeks. Gushing from limestone beds deep within the earth, DePuy, Armstrong's, and Nelson spring creeks are blessed with a nearly constant year-round temperature, a unique chemistry that supports abundant aquatic insects, and a correspondingly large population of wild trout. Coursing through private land, each of the spring creeks requires a daily fee to fish them, which is halved in the fall and winter months. The spring creeks are the primary destination of many visiting summer anglers and a wonderful fall and winter respite for guides, who work them only with landing nets for half the year. The river is almost devoid of anglers at a time when the few catch some of the largest trout

Celebrated outdoor writer Charlie Waterman and his wife Debie on the Yellowstone, a river that has figured largely in their lives for many years.

the Yellowstone will yield all year.

The German brown trout is almost invariably the favorite trout of veteran flyfishers worldwide. And it's no different in Montana, despite the lip service paid to the state's only

A Yellowstone brown trout
comes to the net.

distribution, and their signature orange jaw slashes make them unique and exquisite. The all-American rainbow trout needs no introduction or further accolades unless you've never caught a wild specimen, such as the Yellowstone's. But when it comes down to the finest distinctions among the species of power, endurance, and difficulty to dupe on a fly, the brown trout gets the hat trick. And in the Yellowstone River this German immigrant, *Salmo trutta*, spawns in the fall.

While many Yellowstone brown trout are taken on dry flies and nymphs in the spring and summer, fall flyfishing for browns bears little resemblance. Fall anglers are after large browns, which usually are uninterested in the small morsels that

native trout, the cutthroat. Natives, as cutthroats are called, are a first-class member of the trout family. The willingness of the Yellowstone cutthroat *(Salmo clarki lewisi)* to take an artificial fly, their exclusive western

Dogs make great fishing companions. They're always ready to go and they rarely roll their eyes when the day's big-fish story is told.

artificial dry flies and most nymphs represent. To make a living in the Yellowstone, big browns can't afford to waste energy chasing small flies. These predators need substantial hunks of protein, such as sculpins,

whitefish, and other trout — browns included. To illustrate, several seasons ago I was enjoying catching fall rainbow trout of various sizes from a short, shallow riffle that tailed out into a sizable hole. I was reaching to unhook a 12-inch 'bow when a large form shot upstream from the hole, grabbed the trout crosswise in its jaws and started moving away, almost casually. I put maximum pressure on the 4X tippet just to turn the big brown, which then simply laid in the current a rod length away clenching the rainbow. When I moved the rod again, the big brown turned, swept its broad tail, and simply disappeared downstream into its lair with no more than 2½ inches of rainbow trout protruding from each side of its jaw.

With brown trout like that in the

offing, fall anglers fish big streamer flies in deep holes. The trout, which move upriver as much as thirty miles to spawn, are hungry, distracted by spawning or pre-spawn activities, and are often not well oriented to the river. For once, anglers have an edge. All that remains is to select a day with an imminent threat of rain or snow, wade deep, and cast a sink-tip line into the deepest holes you can find. In other words, it's the Yellowstone's answer to steelhead fishing. It's a game for the stout of heart and sturdy of limb that can pay off in the trout of a lifetime, a 10-pounder or larger. The Yellowstone's browns will continue spawning into late November. Meanwhile, the river's rainbows and cutthroats are on the fin and feasting on the bounty of eggs,

making them the target of flyfishers not bent on tangling with gator browns.

The waning of the brown trout spawn marks yet a different season for the Yellowstone. The rich odor of wood smoke has replaced the nut-brown smell of early autumn. The distant growl of chain saws etching the high country for a winter supply of firewood is stilled. Mallards that were indifferent to the high season's boats and anglers now have hair triggers, leaping into flight at the slightest suspicion that a hunter approaches. The Canada geese, too, keep a watchful distance. A skiff of powder-light snow blankets the region. And the frail beginnings of shelf ice that will soon block the river in slower sections has formed over

Fall trouting has its rewards, such as this brute. Hook a trout like this and you're in for a Nantucket sleigh ride!

Moose are fairly common along the Yellowstone. They always need a wide berth, but especially during the early fall rut.

river rocks bearing the scuff marks of summer's errant drift boats.

Few traces of autumn remain. Indeed, the talk along the river corridor is of trophy elk downed or targeted, limits of migrating geese, and the rising price of hay to get the cattle through the winter. There is little talk of trout and fishing. Even the fly shops, though open, seem more like long-toothed panhandlers now than the hub of activity they were short months ago. A trickle of customers come and go, but few with a bounce in their step. There's the ponderous weight of knowing that winter — Montana winter — is on the way. Still, there are those drawn to the river. Few trout anglers who find themselves on the river in late fall care openly about the "whys" of it, about

a scrupulous examination of inner space. Most know that they would fail every test and risk breaking their last psychic mooring line. Though the Yellowstone's year-round flyfishers are seldom simple, the issue of why and when they fish has long ago bypassed psychic circuit-breakers. It's now the oversimplified but workable private recognition: "I fish therefore I am." When pressed to articulate such passion, the matter becomes further veiled in the pithy but unassailable: "The best time to fish is when you can." And late fall isn't a bad time to wet a line.

Unlike brown trout, which spawn in suitable sections of the main river and its side channels, rainbow trout seek the Yellowstone's feeder streams. Though the main spawn doesn't get under way until January, late fall marks the pre-spawn, a time when the rainbows begin staging in large numbers in the river's deeper riffles. It's the Yellowstone's 16- to 24-inch rainbows that are the primary spawners, but many smaller and some larger 'bows join the soiree. And in each suitable riffle, especially those just downstream of feeder streams, are party crashers clad in the colors of cutthroat and brown trout.

Although the rainbows are responding to biological imperative, they do not go "off the feed" during the pre-spawn. On the contrary, they seem to feed heavily, as if they somehow know that the rigors of the spawn and the winter months ahead will take their toll. The rainbows don't seem any less selective about taking artificial flies during the pre-spawn. And it has been my experience that they in fact take them more readily. Like the Yellowstone's rainbows at any other time of the year, pre-spawners may, for example, reject a Gold-Ribbed Hare's Ear and take a Prince Nymph. But when you discover the fly they want, the trout will compete for it, which doesn't happen often on the Yellowstone. Once the rainbows move upstream and into the feeder streams where the legal fishing season is closed, they are out of the reach of fall anglers, which is as it should be.

Another Yellowstone River resident that comes in to its own during late fall is the mountain whitefish, *Prosopium williamsoni*. Whitefish are the Rodney Dangerfields of Montana.

The Yellowstone River is a cathedral of wilderness for many anglers worldwide.

Because they compete directly with trout for food and often feed and travel in large schools, they frustrate flyfishers, taking artificial dry and wet flies meant for trout with equal gusto. As a result, they get little respect. Some years ago whitefish were given the "Montana handshake" and then tossed on the bank when caught by anglers. But recently they have been given game fish status, allowing them to take artificial flies with some impunity. They aren't usually tossed on the bank these days. Thus is the status of the whitefish during the spring and summer. But that changes markedly in the late fall and winter when their flesh firms in the cold water, making them prime candidates to grace the racks of smoke houses of all shapes and sizes.

Come late fall near most of the towns and settlements along the Yellowstone River, it's uncommon not to see a solitary figure or two working a run with a fly rod for whitefish. These anglers appear to lack the intensity and fervor of trout anglers. But on a regular basis, every few minutes their rod will bow and vibrate with the struggles of a fish. The fish is gently unhooked and dropped into a plastic grocery bag. Then a fresh maggot is impaled on the hook, and the drift begins anew. The figure is one among a sizable cadre of dedicated whitefish anglers that takes its sport seriously. Don't make the mistake of fishing one of their runs for trout when their mysterious omens foretell a whitefish day. They were fishing that run before

A great gray owl takes flight. Owls are one of many species of raptors along the Yellowstone corridor.

you were born, or at least they'll make you believe it. Some whitefish anglers use bait, some use flies only, some tip their flies with bait. That much is known. The more arcane details of the sport, such as the use of split-shot, tippet size, rod length and weight are not widely discussed by its practitioners. But whether you go fishing for whitefish or catch them by happenstance while trout fishing in the fall, when they come out of the smoker, whitefish far transcend the reputation they had going in.

Such is the Yellowstone in the autumn. It's largely a benevolent season that provides the region's inhabitants, humans included, with a gradual transition between summer and winter.

Winter. That longest of all seasons when a cold wraith stalks the land from the prairies to the Rockies, freezing cattle in the fields and ushering in a new fishing year.

Lip-curling, common to all deer in North America, is a rutting behavior. If you see a bull moose displaying such behavior, you're far too close to a dangerous animal.

WINTER

S O OFTEN WINTER in northern climes is described in the darkest terms — the season of death, a time when nature culls that which is not superbly fit to survive the season. Man is the sole exception. Beginning early in the 20th century, technology has largely insulated humankind from this reality. We control our indoor environment. We travel, feed, give birth, and live normal lives, generally unmindful of the season. But this freedom from the verities of season is not enjoyed by wildlife, which must migrate, stockpile food, hibernate, breed and give birth — all on a timetable and in a manner that gives each species the best odds of surviving winter.

Sign tells the story. A grouse was a half-step behind a bird of prey on the banks of the Yellowstone.

By comparison, we have it easy. But that ease comes at the price of dissociation from and complacency toward the natural world.

In the Yellowstone region, winter is a serious matter for both humans and animals. Certainly, its human inhabitants have technological advancements as a buffer. But unlike more populous areas of the nation, bad judgment or even bad luck can prove fatal in Montana. Not a winter passes without a hiker, hunter, back country skier, or a motorist dying of what newspaper headlines euphemistically call "exposure." During a recent winter, a young acquaintance of mine died near Froze to Death Grazing Area, a remote area in eastern Montana. He lost control of his vehicle on an icy dirt road and tried to hike to the closest ranch house. During such winters, animals fare far worse. During the brutal winter of 1996–97 cattle froze in the fields, and the devastating toll on wildlife was only revealed by aerial surveys the following spring.

Against that backdrop it would seem that the Yellowstone and its environs have little to recommend it in the winter. And that trout fishing holds about the same possibilities as a snowball in hell. Neither could be further from the truth.

To be privy to a winter world where man is an obtrusive yet infrequent visitor is an invigorating glimpse at a reality that is no less relevant or important than one's own. Such are the explorer's rewards of the Yellowstone in winter.

Winter is an intimate season on the Yellowstone, one filled with surprise and discovery. The surprises, compared to those of summer, are small — like a flawless diamond. And the thrill of discovery resonates loudly or not, according to the perceptiveness of the discoverer. For example, the detailed impression of wing tips, perfectly preserved in fresh snow, describe a fleeting drama. "Sign," an ancient term that refers to the tell-tale passing of prey, is everywhere, and more succinct and telling than the words themselves. The grouse, whose flush is preserved in the snow, knew it was being hunted. Its meandering feeding trail through clumps of balsam, whose berries are its favorite winter food, is interrupted by a wide circle of its tracks as the

The few. The solitary. The obsessed.

game bird checked behind it, suspicious. The nearby tracks of a coyote, distinct by their size and unretractable claw marks, are screened by balsam bush. After circling, the grouse hunkered down in the snow to make

itself less visible to the predator it now knew was on its trail. Facing away, the grouse gave the coyote the chance to get within striking range, which it did by staying low, its chest dragging in the snow, to bushes a leap away. Sensing imminent danger, the grouse stood, paced in a tight circle, coiled in the snow, and sprang into flight. The coyote, too, sprang, closing the distance in one motion and leaping into the air to catch the grouse in its jaws. Efficient in every way, the coyote left nothing but a few tail feathers.

But not all of the Yellowstone's surprises and special moments are known only though sign. A band of antelope running the high benches of the Absarokas at midnight, their legs concealed by a mist of fine snow,

Mallards Rest, one of the Yellowstone's many public accesses in Paradise Valley.

appear to float, lean, and turn as one, in characteristic single-file. Were it not for the rhythmic bobbing of their heads, visible by the light of a half-moon, they would appear to be speeding carousel figures in a giant theme park.

Even in the depths of winter, the Yellowstone can suddenly erupt in a hatch of *Baetis* or midges and rising trout.

And sometimes the Yellowstone reveals a ruthless nature on such a scale as to be overwhelming. A lone buffalo, beyond his prime and forced from the herd, crosses one of the Yellowstone's many frozen sloughs. The ice cracks and gives way beneath the bull's tremendous weight. Terrified, his eyes bulging to their whites, the bull struggles for purchase on the edge of the ice with hooves unfit for the purpose. This he does again and again, grunting in protest and effort, his great head a latticework of ice. With one final heave, twin plumes of exhausted breath stream into the cold, still air and the buffalo holds himself half out of the river, his massive shoulders quivering from the effort. But it's not enough. He falls backward with a baleful groan and slips under the ice. Hours later winter has erased all evidence of the bison's struggle.

For the angler, winter marks the height of the rainbow trout spawn. Many 'bows are in tributaries and on their redds in January, February, and March. And many more are in the Yellowstone's frigid flows, staging for the spawn or simply following the migration of their brethren. It's now when winter has the Yellowstone in its tightest grip. Shelf ice spans the river where the flows are moderate. At sharp bends in the river, snow and ice cover the Yellowstone, transforming it into a forbidding moonscape of jumbled tons of upthrust ice floes. On the coldest of days these ice jams expand to their maximum and emit shuddering groans as though they were a living thing. In counterpoint,

Winter nymphing on the
Yellowstone.

conifers literally explode with the loudness of a rifle shot as their sap freezes and expands beyond the tree's ability to contain it.

Trout fishing in such conditions? No. But what makes fishing possible are the Chinooks that blow through the region, raising the temperature from well below zero to the mid-40s or higher. During a typical winter this freeze-and-thaw cycle occurs at ten-day intervals; a week of cold followed by three days of mild Chinook weather. It's during Chinooks that the Yellowstone becomes eminently fish-able, to the point of offering dry-fly fishing. Like late fall, wading the Yellowstone in the winter isn't to be taken lightly. But winter fishing is often easier than fishing in the fall, because the river is at its absolute low-est flows of the year and thick shelf ice often extends to the edges of the best runs. As a result, wading is often unnecessary. Chinooks do weaken the ice, so winter anglers should heed Shakespeare's advice: "Discretion is the better part of valor."

A situation in which I was involv-ed several seasons ago illustrates the quality of the Yellowstone's winter fishing and the nature of its shelf ice. Despite the bitter temperatures, rainbow trout were spawning in the river's back channels and feeder streams in water too shallow to cover their backs and dorsal fins. The cold had lingered for two weeks, limiting outdoor activity to only that which was essential. Elk streamed out of the high country black timber to bask in the meager sun that bathed the

THE FUTURE

I F WE ARE INDEED plucking the goose that laid the golden egg, at least its flight feathers remain intact. "As long as the Yellowstone's headwaters are protected the river will hold up as a quality fishery," predicts John Bailey. Fortunately, the Yellowstone's headwaters lie largely within an area protected from development, agricultural runoff, overgrazing by domestic stock, and a host of other banes of wild trout in Yellowstone National Park.

The Greater Yellowstone Coalition's Dennis Glick agrees. But he cautions that without a comprehensive plan that considers the Yellowstone's entire watershed, the river and its

Dennis Glick

trout will suffer. "Right now the Yellowstone is a classic example of death by a thousand cuts," Glick says. To correct that, he says, "We're going to have to broaden our view and think about the cumulative impact of everything that is affecting the river." Some of the major steps Glick listed to stop the degradation of the Yellowstone are restricting commercial logging on Forest Service land, establishing construction set-backs and county zoning favorable to the river, restricting mining in the Yellowstone watershed, and keeping cattle away from riparian zones.

Those are tall orders in Montana and in the West where, as Glick says, "Private property rights are sacrosanct regardless of the effect they may have on the environment." Indeed, at the core of western land-use philosophy — one that evolved through the efforts of generations of settlers — is that people do whatever is necessary to protect their land, home, stock, and family. That creed is directly responsible for the extirpation of wolves in Yellowstone National Park by 1926 and the great local resistance to restocking them in 1995 to re-establish a wild population. It is also directly responsible for the actions of Montana Department of Livestock agents in gunning down scores of buffalo that wander out of the park in search of food each winter. Private-property rights have a full set of teeth in Montana. Against such a backdrop, can there be any positive prognosis for the Yellowstone River?

"The Yellowstone region has a

mystic, international reputation and it's the river that ties it all together," says John Bailey. "And I think people know that they need to maintain the river as a whole to maintain the region's integrity." Glick, too, puts a certain measure of faith in our need for wild places. "The one thing that gives me a great deal of hope is that people living along the river value the Yellowstone as a unique and valuable resource," he said.

One can only hope that Bailey and Glick are right. But such hope is weak tea in the face of rampant development and the apparent inability or lack of local will to control it for the river's sake. In a recent Livingston/Park County meeting to consider riparian-protection measures along the

Yellowstone, one of the most prominent and influential residents of Paradise Valley voiced strong opposition to any "county zoning." It appears that if there is to be any protection of the Yellowstone, it will

Will the next generation of anglers inherit a legacy of wild Yellowstone River trout? Decisions being made now hold the answer.

Efforts begun a decade ago to restore pure-strain Yellowstone cutthroat trout are beginning to pay off.

halt the park's winter buffalo slaughter.

That is not to say that the Yellowstone River and its trout are being left to fend for themselves. With more fishing guides and outfitters than any other region of Montana, Livingston and Park County have a burgeoning fishing industry that cares deeply about the Yellowstone. I do not personally know of a single guide or outfitter who allows clients to kill the trout they catch in the Yellowstone. And while guided trips account for only 16 percent of the fishing pressure on the river, it is equally unusual to see unguided flyfishers keeping their trout. Such enlightened practices go a long way toward protecting wild trout, but they do not go far enough.

have to be prompted largely by interest groups and individuals who don't live in the region, as was the case with stopping the New World Mine, reintroducing wolves to Yellowstone Park, and attempts to

A bait-fishing ban on the Yellowstone River's trout water, as exists in Yellowstone National Park, and a further single-hook restriction on artificial lures would be of great benefit to the fishery.

Several years ago I was guiding clients on an artificial-only section of the Yellowstone River. We pulled in for lunch where a nonresident angler with a spinning rod was fighting a large trout. I netted the fish for the man, a brown trout of 20 inches that weighed 3½ pounds or so. While landing the trophy, I noticed that the angler had illegally caught the trout on a nightcrawler. Ignoring my protests, he unceremoniously slid the trout into a bag on the bank that contained three others like it. "I've been coming here to fish for twenty years and the fishing sure has dropped off," was his only comment.

So while the majority of the trout-fishing community has made great strides toward the preservation of wild fish, there remain many who

Unspoiled views and superb trout fishing have long been taken for granted on the Yellowstone.

Year-round Yellowstone River residents, common mergansers thrive on the river's smaller trout and whitefish.

Yellowstone's largest trout. It caused a great gnashing of teeth when sculpins were identified as a carrier of Whirling Disease. Their use as live bait was subsequently halted on the Yellowstone and other Montana rivers.

Guides, outfitters, and conscientious anglers are most effective at protecting and preserving the fishery as it exists. When it comes to the larger land-use issues that affect the fishery, anglers may weigh in, but they're perceived as a special-interest group that is not representative of the whole. And the "whole" is, at least for the moment and at least locally, an unknown quantity in terms of the Yellowstone's fate.

So the river appears to face one of two fates. Without intervention in the near future the Yellowstone River

see the resource for consumptive use. Indeed, until 1996 and a state-wide Whirling Disease scare, it was common practice locally to seine "bullheads" or sculpin in the river and use them as live bait for the

corridor will become increasingly populated by rural subdivisions that will greatly detract from its appeal. The trout fishing, though not currently at serious risk from development, will suffer first esthetically. As the Greater Yellowstone Coalition's Dennis Glick says, "You'll still be able to catch trout, but you'll be catching them in someone's backyard." Already, other outfitters in the region and I have begun to avoid stretches of the river where the heretofore unobstructed views of the flanking Absaroka and Gallatin mountains are blocked by summer homes on the river's banks.

Alternatively, the Yellowstone could become the beneficiary of enlightened policies that protect and preserve it as the national treasure that it truly is — a future it richly deserves.

The Yellowstone River flows through several ecosystems between Yellowstone Park and its confluence with the Missouri.

A FEW TIPS AND TACTICS

THIS BOOK IS NOT meant to be a treatise on flyfishing techniques for the Yellowstone River. But it would no doubt be incomplete without an overview of some of the advanced tactics for catching the river's trout. And since the vast majority of anglers fish the Yellowstone in the summer, let's focus our attention there.

Quality equipment for fishing the Yellowstone is the same as it is anywhere. It's just that it's likely to be tested to its limit on the Yellowstone.

First, come to the region equipped to fish a big western river. Beyond basic equipment, that includes:

- A 9-foot rod for a 5-, 6-, or 7-weight line
- A quality fly reel
- Polarized sunglasses
- Lightweight waders and felt-bottom wading shoes
- A stomach pump
- A wading staff
- A small backpack for carrying water and snacks
- Sunscreen rated at SPF 15 or higher
- A small seine, such as an aquarium net
- A lightweight camera

Assuming that this is an unguided fishing vacation, the first thing to do is check in with one of the area's flyfishing shops. Dan Bailey's Fly Shop and George Anderson's Yellowstone Angler in Livingston are first-rate. If you plan to fish the river in Yellowstone National Park, stop in at Richard Park's Fly Shop in Gardiner. Check the hatch board to see what the trout are taking on various sections of the river. Then ask one of the clerks to put a "guide box" together, a selection of the flies you're likely to need.

Unless you're an inveterate fly-tier, buy your flies when you arrive. Most trout flies in Montana are tied for a specific river and don't travel well, even from river to river in the state.

After you have selected a stretch of the Yellowstone to fish, assemble and carry with you everything that you'll need for the entire day. In making your choice of where to fish, give top consideration to the main river's inside bends and riverside channels. In Montana, anglers have access to the high-water mark. Do not cross private land to get to the river. Use the many public accesses that are clearly marked on maps and road signs. And wherever you enter the river, plan on fishing on that side of the river only. There are very few places where wading anglers can cross the Yellowstone safely.

When you start fishing, before your first cast pay close attention to activity along the bank upstream. Check nearby bushes for caddisflies.

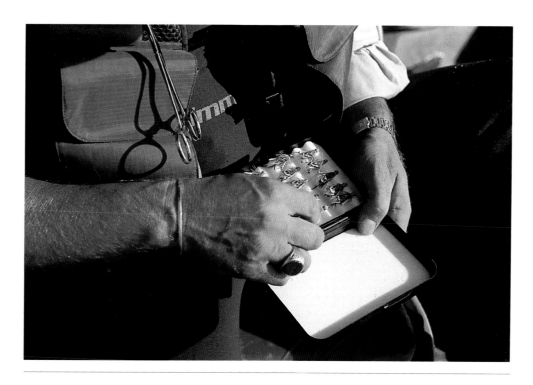

Note if there are any rising fish and determine the fly they're rising to. If there is no surface activity, bugs or fish, use your seine to determine which nymphs are in the current. Then match them with an imitation

If it's summer on the Yellowstone, it's 'hopper season.

A FEW TIPS AND TACTICS

The Stimulator is a fly pattern that floats extremely well in the Yellowstone's turbulent flows and suggests several of its trouts' favorite foods, including grasshoppers.

day. As soon as the temperature rises to the point where it's hot, start looking and listening for grasshopper activity. In fact, it's such a foregone conclusion that the trout will start looking up for 'hoppers that it's best to tie one on and start fishing it. Start with smaller 'hoppers, size 10s and 12s, and increase the size of your offering as the day warms. Grasshoppers are cold-blooded and the smaller insects become active first.

Cast 'hoppers along the bank as you proceed upstream. Like all trout, Yellowstone trout prefer to lie just upstream or downstream of obstructions that break the current, usually rocks. With a 9-foot 4X leader tied on, investigate each likely spot. If it's early in the 'hopper activity, a dry fly or nymph dropper

of the approximate size, shape, and color.

Whatever may or may not be happening on the Yellowstone when you start fishing in the morning, bear in mind that it's going to be a 'hopper

can be productive. To set up a dropper, simply tie 1½ to 2 feet of tippet material to the bend of the 'hopper with an improved clinch knot and tie the dropper fly to the end. If the trout take the 'hopper you'll know it. If they take the dropper, the 'hopper becomes the strike indicator.

Visiting anglers will have no problem setting the hook on the Yellowstone's brown and rainbow trout. But its cutthroat trout are an entirely different matter. Cutts rise slowly, with confidence, engulfing the fly. They then turn and head back to their feeding lie. It's important to refrain from setting the hook until the cutt turns. Otherwise you'll often pull the 'hopper pattern right out of the fish's mouth. It's a fine point but a telling point about fishing for

Dave Corcoran, owner of Bozeman's River's Edge fly shop, with his fishing partner and a fine Yellowstone trout.

cutthroat. And you'll see what I mean with your first take.

When you hook a large trout in the Yellowstone, take your time fighting it. The river's trout know exactly how to use the Yellowstone's

A FEW TIPS AND TACTICS

'Hoppers are synonymous with summer on the Yellowstone. Most years, the Yellowstone has the most dependable 'hopper "hatch" and resulting topwater fishing of any Montana river.

currents to their full advantage. Get the trout on the reel as quickly as possible and then trust your rod and reel. Follow the fish downstream if you can and get it near the bank, out of the main current. Avoid reeling the

line/leader knot through the rod guides. A big Yellowstone trout invariably will make one last run, and a nail knot in the rod guides spells a broken tippet. Take a photo of your trophy and then revive it in calm water for about as long as you fought the trout.

As the day winds down and cools, adjust your fishing techniques accordingly. That means ending the day as you began it, with smaller flies — a Parachute Adams, an Al Troth Caddis, or maybe a nymph or emerger. Again, cold-blooded grasshoppers slow or cease their daily activity when the air temperature falls.

At the end of the day, check in with the fly shop and tell them how you did, and buy a replacement fly or two. Make your plan for the